The World's Greatest Leader ... Ever!

Exploring the Gospel of Luke

This book belongs to ....

I am .... (Age)

People sometimes call me .... (My Nickname)

I live at ....

....

The Bible is alive!

It's alive with personalities, stories, events, ideas, news … alive with God's involvement with people and the world he made. It's about people and for people – even quite young people.

This book is one of a series of *Hotshots* books designed to help children enjoy reading the Bible. The series has been creatively and carefully planned as an introduction to some of the characters, events and teachings of the Bible. It is pitched at the child's level of understanding and enjoyment to show how the ageless Book relates to the child's world of the here and now.

There are 60 sections covering a large proportion of Luke's Gospel. The Bible passages are included in *Hotshots* so the children can access them easily. The version quoted is the *Contemporary English Version*, widely recommended as an ideal modern version for children and adults alike. It is available from the Bible Society quite inexpensively.

Hotshots contains things to think about, projects to do, skills to learn. A few questions or projects will require your help and attention. We hope these will provide natural spots for stimulating family interactions and encouragement.

This book introduces children to Jesus as presented by Luke so they can begin to discover the personality, teaching and saving work of this central figure of all history.

It is our prayer that through this book, the children will begin to love the Bible and become familiar with it. We also prayerfully hope that the children will begin to take steps towards Jesus in ways that will lead them to a maturing faith as they grow older.

Getting Started with Hotshots

The Bible is a large book. Where will you begin? *Hotshots* makes starting easier.

Choose when and where to do your *Hotshots* reading.

I'm going to read Hotshots each morning. So I don't forget anything I will make an audio cassette on my tape recorder.

Keep handy:

- A pen
- Scissors
- Coloured pencils

I will do my Hotshots when I get home from school. I will write important things in a notebook.

Now decide:

What time is best for you?

....

Where?

....

Where will I write important things?

....

I'm going to read Hotshots before I go to bed. I'll be putting my ideas on my computer.

Meet the HOTSHOTS

Kim

Anna

They're a Sensation!

Our basketball club always dreams of winning … and having fun. They meet Jeff, their leader, every Friday night for basketball practice, burgers and coke and a chat about the Bible. Sometimes they watch a video or cook some food or tell jokes!

Hong

They love Fridays with their friend Jeff. He's the tallest guy they've seen!

Samuel

Emily

Dan

Chris

Jeff

The Hotshots read the Bible ...

... you can too! We have included here the parts of the Bible you need and some *Hotshots* puzzles and things to think about.

The Bible bits come from the Gospel of Luke (sometimes called 'Good News by Luke').

The Bible has chapters and verses to help you find your place and we use a 'reference' like this:

The book of the Bible	*The chapter: Chapter 5*	*The verses: verses 1 to 3*
↓	↓	↓

Luke 5:1-3

Look in the 'Contents Page' near the start of the Bible to find Luke, the third book in the New Testament part of the Bible.

Try this fun test.

Luke 1:26

The name of the angel who visited Mary

G						

Luke 4:16

The town where Jesus was brought up

N								

Show this book to your parents. Ask them to help you read it and answer your questions.

Who is Luke?

Luke 1:1-4

[1] Many people have tried to tell the story of what God has done among us. [2] They wrote what we had been told by the ones who were there in the beginning and saw what happened. [3] So I made a careful study of everything and then decided to write and tell you exactly what took place. Honorable Theophilus, [4] I have done this to let you know the truth about what you have heard.

Prayer: *Dear God, please help me to learn lots about Jesus in this Hotshots book.*

Yesterday one of my friends told us a joke. But the problem was, he got the ending confused. The joke wasn't funny any more!

Luke was a doctor. Many of the stories going around about Jesus were mixed up. So Luke wanted to make sure people found out the true story of Jesus.

Is this report correct? (Look at the Bible verses again and write a ✓ or a ✗ beside each sentence.)

☐ Luke was a doctor

☐ He wrote to Theophilus – an important Roman official.

☐ Theophilus knew a little about Jesus

☐ Luke wrote his gospel in a hurry.

(Answers next page. ✓ = True; ✗ = False.)

Prayer: *Thank you God that Luke worked very carefully to write down his story of Jesus.*

Just the facts!

Luke 3:1-2

[1] For 15 years Emperor Tiberius had ruled that part of the world. Pontius Pilate was governor of Judea, and Herod was the ruler of Galilee. Herod's brother, Philip, was the ruler in the countries of Iturea and Trachonitis, and Lysanias was the ruler of Abilene. [2] Annas and Caiaphas were the Jewish high priests. At that time God spoke to Zechariah's son John, who was living in the desert.

Prayer: Thank you for the true story of Jesus.

How do we know Luke told his story correctly?

What names! They are hard to say, but help us to know exactly when and where Jesus lived. Well done Luke!

Read the verses again. Match the names to the correct job. (*We've done the first to give you a start.*)

Annas	Emperor of Rome
Caiaphas	Governor of Judea
Tiberius	Ruler of Galilee
Philip	Ruler of Iturea
Herod	Ruler of Abilene
Lysanius	High Priest
Pontius Pilate	High Priest

Ask your parents to help you find something in an encyclopedia about Emperor Tiberius. *What was his first name?*

Answer to puzzle on page 6 : ✓,✓,✓,X.

3 More stories from Dr Luke

[1] Theophilus, I first wrote to you about all that Jesus did and taught from the very first [2] until he was taken up to heaven. But before he was taken up, he gave orders to the apostles he had chosen with the help of the Holy Spirit. [3] For 40 days after Jesus had suffered and died, he proved in many ways that he had been raised from death. He appeared to his apostles and spoke to them about God's kingdom.

A *sequel* is a story that continues on to another book.

My spooky story isn't finished. I had to borrow the next part from the library.

THE HAUNTED HOUSE MYSTERY

THE SQUEAKY DOOR - SEQUEL TO THE HAUNTED HOUSE MYSTERY

The Book of Acts in the Bible is the *sequel* to the Gospel of Luke. It continues on with the story. Luke wrote both books.

Who did Dr Luke write his story for?

See verse 1. The Book of Acts starts where the Gospel of Luke ends. Tick the story that ends the Gospel of Luke.

- [ ] Jesus is killed
- [ ] Jesus is taken up to heaven
- [ ] Jesus is arrested by soldiers.

Prayer: I am sorry that Jesus suffered and died but I'm glad he came alive again.

Joining the team

When the kids wanted to join Hotshots they came to practice. Then they signed some papers and got their team uniform to show that they belonged.

In a similar way, people are baptised today as a sign of belonging to Jesus' team. Even Jesus was baptised to start his work.

Luke 3:21-23

21While everyone else was being baptised, Jesus himself was baptised. Then as he prayed, the sky opened up, 22 and the Holy Spirit came down upon him in the form of a dove. A voice from heaven said, "You are my own dear Son, and I am pleased with you." When Jesus began to preach, he was about 30 years old.

With a red marker pen, underline the words that show how God felt about Jesus.

Do you know anyone who is the same age as Jesus when he began his work?

Do you remember the day you joined Hotshots? It was the day you got your uniforms!

Prayer: *Please help me to understand how to be part of Jesus' team.*

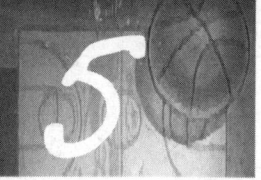

A very special person

Luke 4:16-20

[16] Jesus went back to Nazareth, where he had been brought up, and as usual he went to the meeting place on the Sabbath. When he stood up to read from the Scriptures, [17] he was given the book of Isaiah the prophet. He opened it and read,

> [18] "The Lord's Spirit has come to me,
>> because he has chosen me
>> to tell the good news to the poor.
>
> The Lord has sent me
>> to announce freedom for prisoners,
>> to give sight to the blind,
>> to free everyone who suffers,
>
> [19] and to say, 'This is the year the Lord has chosen.'"

[20] Jesus closed the book, then handed it back to the man in charge and sat down.

The neighbours thought they knew Jesus. He grew up with them. When Jesus said, "These are the words Isaiah wrote over 600 years ago… and today they have come true!" SURPRISE. Suddenly their neighbour was a very special leader.

Our neighbour used to be just ordinary. Now he's the captain of the Knights basketball team!

What special things would this leader do? (Draw lines to join the correct round bits to the square bits.)

Good news for…	the blind
Sight for…	prisoners
Freedom for…	the poor

Prayer: *Please God, help me to understand how special Jesus is.*

What people thought

²² All the people started talking about Jesus and were amazed at the wonderful things he said. They kept on asking, "Isn't he Joseph's son?"
²⁸ When the people in the meeting place heard Jesus say this, they became so angry ²⁹ that they got up and threw him out of town. They dragged him to the edge of the cliff on which the town was built, because they wanted to throw him down from there.
³⁰ But Jesus slipped through the crowd and got away.

What did the people think of Jesus? Different people thought different things. Underline the words in colour.

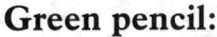

We were surprised because we knew him when he was a kid.

Red pencil:
'We were amazed that Jesus' words were so powerful and true.'

Blue pencil:
'We were surprised because we knew him when he was a kid.'

Green pencil:
'We were angry. Let's kill him.'

Look in a mirror and pull these faces for fun.

- Look like the angry crowd.
- Look like Jesus teaching.
- Look like someone sitting in the crowd.

Prayer: *Dear God, please remind me often about how special Jesus is.*

We were angry! Let's kill him!

Amaaaazing!

Prayer: *Dear God, when I read stories about Jesus long ago, help me to see what I should think today.*

Luke 5:1-11

[1] Jesus was standing on the shore of Lake Gennesaret, teaching the people as they crowded around him to hear God's message.

[2] Near the shore he saw two boats left there by some fishermen who had gone to wash their nets. [3] Jesus ... told Simon, "Row the boat out into the deep water and let your nets down to catch some fish."

[5] "Master," Simon answered, "we have worked hard all night long and have not caught a thing. But if you tell me to, I will let the nets down." [6] They did it and caught so many fish that their nets began ripping apart.

[8] When Simon Peter saw this happen, he knelt down in front of Jesus and said, "Lord, don't come near me! I am a sinner." [9] Peter and everyone with him were completely surprised at all the fish they had caught.

[10] Jesus told Simon, "Don't be afraid! From now on you will bring in people instead of fish." [11] The men pulled their boats up on the shore. Then they left everything and went with Jesus.

LAKE

Write the name of the Lake on the sign

How did Simon Peter feel when he caught so many fish? (Read verse 8 and tick **one** box.)

☐ Very pleased and proud.

☐ Not good enough to be Jesus' friend.

☐ Very curious.

Simon Peter found out Jesus was much greater than he guessed. This embarrassed him.

He remembered the things he'd done wrong in his life (what the Bible calls sin). But Jesus said 'Cheer up! I want you to be my friend. We've got work do.'

Prayer: Thank you Jesus, that you want me to be your friend and follower too.

Last night I watched league basketball. I saw the most amazing slam dunk! It was so good I wanted to record it and watch it over and over and over. It was too good to be true!

SLAM!

A sick and anxious man

People in Jesus' time were quite scared of skin diseases like leprosy. If they didn't get better the people had to leave home and live alone outside. They must have felt very alone and afraid. Maybe what they most needed was a hug from someone.

My guinea pig had a skin disease. The Vet told me to put on ointment and keep it away from my other guinea pig in case he caught it.

Luke 5:12-13

¹²Jesus came to a town where there was a man who had leprosy. When the man saw Jesus, he knelt down to the ground in front of Jesus and begged, "Lord, you have the power to make me well, if only you wanted to." ¹³ Jesus put his hand on him and said, "I want to! Now you are well." At once the man's leprosy disappeared.

What did Jesus do for the man?
Look at verse 13. Tick the correct answer.

☐ Kept his distance like everyone else
☐ Healed the man from a long way away
☐ Touched the man to make him better.

The man was anxious about his disease but Jesus healed him in a very loving way.

Can you decode this message?

JESUSLOVESMEANDCARESFORMEINLOVINGWAYS

Draw lines to mark where the spaces between the words should be.

Prayer: Thank you Jesus that you understand how I feel. When I'm lonely and afraid help me to remember that you love me.

The wheelchair man

I saw on TV people in wheelchairs playing basketball. They were very fast even though their legs don't work.

In the days of Jesus, wheelchairs had not been invented. Disabled people had to stay on a mat. They needed friends to help them go anywhere. Read about a lucky man with kind friends who met with Jesus.

Luke 5:17-26

[17] One day some Pharisees and experts in the Law of Moses sat listening to Jesus teach.

God had given Jesus the power to heal the sick, [18] and some people came carrying a crippled man on a mat. They tried to take him inside the house and put him in front of Jesus. [19] But because of the crowd, they could not get him to Jesus. So they went up on the roof, where they removed some tiles and let the mat down in the middle of the room.

[20] When Jesus saw how much faith they had, he said to the crippled man, "My friend, your sins are forgiven." [21] The Pharisees and the experts began arguing, "Jesus must think he is God! Only God can forgive sins."

[24] Jesus then said to the man, "Get up! Pick up your mat and walk home."

[25] At once the man stood up in front of everyone. He picked up his mat and went home, giving thanks to God.

[26] Everyone was amazed and praised God. What they saw surprised them, and they said, "We have seen a great miracle today!"

Continued overpage

The wheelchair man (continued...)

Imagine the scene.
Draw what is happening on the roof in the picture.

What was the first thing Jesus said to the man? (tick one)

☐ Why did they wreck the roof?
☐ I forgive the wrong things in your life.
☐ I'm too busy to help you.
☐ Do you want me to heal you?

The teachers believed that only God was allowed to forgive people in this way. Ordinary people didn't have that right. Jesus showed he had the same right as God to forgive sins.

Can you read this code message?

EJESUST JCANE AFORGIVER KMEL SANDY STAKER SMYL KSINE TAWAYN.

Cross out the first and last letters in each word.

Prayer: *Thank you Jesus that you can forgive me and take the wrong things from my life.*

Friends nobody wants

It's not fair! Why do we have to pay basketball club fees?

If you don't pay you can't be part of the team.

Luke 5:27-32

27 Later, Jesus went out and saw a tax collector named Levi sitting at the place for paying taxes. Jesus said to him, "Come with me." 28 Levi left everything and went with Jesus.

29 In his home Levi gave a big dinner for Jesus. Many tax collectors and other guests were also there.

30 The Pharisees and some of their teachers of the Law of Moses grumbled to Jesus' disciples, "Why do you eat and drink with those tax collectors and other sinners?" 31 Jesus answered, "Healthy people don't need a doctor, but sick people do. 32 I didn't come to invite good people to turn to God. I came to invite sinners."

People used to say, 'Don't trust tax men. Avoid them.' But Jesus made a point of getting to know the tax men and enjoyed their company.

Prayer: Please Jesus help me to be kind to

_____.

They don't have many friends. (Think of someone you know.)

Paying club fees is a bit like paying a tax. Taxes are paid to the government and no one likes paying taxes. These people felt the taxmen were stealing some of the money and did not trust them. But Jesus trusted one of them!

What matters most

Samuel is excited because the Hotshots are going on a campout overnight.

One day, Jesus had to decide what was the most important thing he had to do that day.

Luke 6:6-11

⁶ On another Sabbath Jesus was teaching in a Jewish meeting place, and a man with a crippled right hand was there. ⁷ Some Pharisees and teachers of the Law of Moses kept watching Jesus to see if he would heal the man. They did this because they wanted to accuse Jesus of doing something wrong.

⁸ Jesus knew what they were thinking. So he told the man to stand up where everyone could see him. And the man stood up. ⁹ Then Jesus asked, "On the Sabbath should we do good deeds or evil deeds? Should we save someone's life or destroy it?"

¹⁰ After he had looked around at everyone, he told the man, "Stretch out your hand." He did, and his bad hand became completely well.

¹¹ The teachers and the Pharisees were furious and started saying to each other, "What can we do about Jesus?"

The leaders (called 'teachers of the Law' and 'Pharisees') had strict rules about what you could do on the 'Sabbath' day (our Saturday) when people went to worship services. They forced people to keep their rules. Healing was not allowed!

What mattered most?

☐ Healing a person who has not been able to use his right hand for a long time.

☐ Keeping the leaders' rules about the Sabbath day.

Jesus saw that the leaders did not care about this man. They were just trying to trap Jesus. He loved the man and decided it was more important to make the man better, even though it made the leaders mad.

This is the inside of the Jewish meeting place. Draw Jesus and the man.

Prayer: Thank you Jesus that you care about people. Thank you for loving me and caring for me.

12 Friends with a job

The campout was a great success.

Write down what Kim and Dan thought of it.

Jesus knew that his followers would learn lots from him as they travelled everywhere.

Luke 6:12-16

[12] About that time Jesus went off to a mountain to pray, and he spent the whole night there.

[13] The next morning he called his disciples together and chose twelve of them to be his apostles. [14] One was Simon, and Jesus named him Peter. Another was Andrew, Peter's brother. There were also James, John, Philip, Bartholomew, [15] Matthew, Thomas, and James the son of Alphaeus. The rest of the apostles were Simon, known as the Eager One, [16] Jude, who was the son of James, and Judas Iscariot, who later betrayed Jesus.

Jesus prayed before he chose his followers. They were called 'apostles' because Jesus trained them to do a special job. They were all different and it wasn't easy to live together. They learned a lot by travelling and working with Jesus.

Prayer: Please help me Jesus to know how to be your friend and follow you.

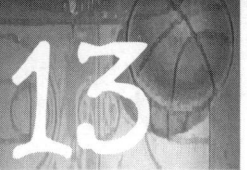

13

Friends for always

Jesus' followers, the 'apostles', were sometimes called 'disciples' or learners.

Luke 8:1-3

¹ Soon after this, Jesus was going through towns and villages, telling the good news about God's kingdom. His twelve apostles were with him, ² and so were some women who had been healed of evil spirits and all sorts of diseases. One of the women was Mary Magdalene, who once had seven demons in her.

³ Joanna, Susanna, and many others had also used what they owned to help Jesus and his disciples. Joanna's husband Chuza was one of Herod's officials.

Some of the disciples were women – some were men.

We can't leave our homes like they did but we can still be 'disciples'! We can be Jesus' friends and learn to be like him. (Just like the Hotshots are learning to play basketball from Jeff.)

Continued overpage

Friends for always

(continued ...)

Have you ever thought about being Jesus' friend? You may like to turn to page 94 and 95 to find out how to do this.

Another code message.

JES USST ILLWA
NTSU STOB EHI
SFRIEN DSFO REVER

The words are divided in the wrong places. Draw lines where the gaps should be.

Prayer: *Jesus please help me to understand how to start and keep on being your friend.'*

Hotshots training session

Catching and throwing

Are you good at catching and throwing? Practising will help. Here are some training tips as you practise with a friend.

1. Enjoy holding a ball. Get to know the ball well! Bounce on the floor and catch, bounce and catch. Throw it up and catch. Keep going till you can catch it every time.

2. Stand with your feet apart – as far as your shoulders.

3. Bend your knees a bit so you are ready to move.

4. Hold your head up and keep looking around.

The learning begins

The Hotshots are unhappy.

There is trouble in the team.

Kim and Anna are angry with each other and have stopped being friends.

Luke 6:27,28,35

27 This is what I say to all who will listen to me: "Love your enemies, and be good to everyone who hates you. 28 Ask God to bless anyone who curses you, and pray for everyone who is cruel to you. 35 But love your enemies and be good to them. Lend without expecting to be paid back. Then you will get a great reward, and you will be the true children of God in heaven. He is good even to people who are unthankful and cruel."

Jesus' disciples were learning surprising new things each day. His ways may be difficult but they are the best ways.

When Kim finishes reading the Bible verses for today, what should she try to do? (Tick one answer.)

☐ Get the other Hotshots to be on her side.

☐ Make Anna feel very uncomfortable.

☐ Tell Anna she's sorry for fighting.

Prayer: *Jesus, please help me to get on well with my friends.*

15

More to learn

The Hotshots are still unhappy.

The troubles are not yet over. Kim and Anna are trying to learn to be friends again.

Luke 6:37-38

37 Jesus said: "Don't judge others, and God won't judge you. Don't be hard on others, and God won't be hard on you. Forgive others, and God will forgive you.

38 The way you treat others is the way you will be treated."

It is easy to judge and be hard on someone else. It is not always easy to feel how they feel. The troubles in the Hotshots needs someone to stop being angry and to take the first step to be friendly.

Now what should Anna do?

☐ Refuse to talk to Kim.

☐ Tell Kim: It's OK. Let's be friends.

☐ Try to make Kim feel terrible.

Maybe there is a person you know who needs you to be a forgiving friend. So you won't forget it decorate verse 28 on page 23 with your coloured pencils.

Prayer: Jesus help me to learn your lessons today.

16 The dinner party

One thing about being on a team is you learn to treat each other with respect ...

... whispering about each other is out!

This dinner party story is about two people.

A man – he was important. Everyone said how good he was. **A woman** – everyone whispered about her. They said she was no good.

Luke 7:36-39

36 A Pharisee invited Jesus to have dinner with him. So Jesus went to the Pharisee's home and got ready to eat.

37 When a sinful woman in that town found out that Jesus was there, she bought an expensive bottle of perfume. 38 Then she came and stood behind Jesus. She cried and started washing his feet with her tears and drying them with her hair. The woman kissed his feet and poured the perfume on them.

39 The Pharisee who had invited Jesus saw this and said to himself, "If this man really were a prophet, he would know what kind of woman is touching him! He would know that she is a sinner."

The two people in our story were both kind to Jesus. One invited Jesus to dinner, the other gave Jesus a very special gift. Which one, do you think, most wanted to show love for Jesus? (Choose the answer when you read the rest of the story on the next page.)

Prayer: Jesus I love you very much. Please help me to love you more.

After the dinner party

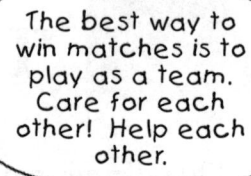

The best way to win matches is to play as a team. Care for each other! Help each other.

Remember the man who was important and the woman everyone thought was no good? Who loved Jesus most? Read on.

Luke 7:44-50

44 He turned toward the woman and said to Simon, "Have you noticed this woman? When I came into your home, you didn't give me any water so I could wash my feet. But she has washed my feet with her tears and dried them with her hair. 45 You didn't greet me with a kiss, but from the time I came in, she has not stopped kissing my feet. 46 You didn't even pour olive oil on my head, but she has poured expensive perfume on my feet. 47 So I tell you that all her sins are forgiven, and that is why she has shown great love. But anyone who has been forgiven for only a little will show only a little love."

48 Then Jesus said to the woman, "Your sins are forgiven."

49 Some other guests started saying to one another, "Who is this who dares to forgive sins?" 50 But Jesus told the woman, "Because of your faith, you are now saved. May God give you peace!"

Did the important man care for his visitor Jesus? Write down something he didn't do for him?

_____

Did the woman care for Jesus? Write down something she did for him.

_____

Prayer: *Lord Jesus please help me to think of a way to show you I love you. (You may like to ask your parents what they think about this.)*

18

When bad things happen

Samuel tripped and fell on a step while he was running to Hotshots practice. He had a broken leg. He felt scared about going to the Hospital Emergency Clinic.

Bad things can happen to anyone. Following Jesus doesn't stop bad things happening. Even the disciples had a frightening experience.

Luke 8:22-25

[22] One day, Jesus and his disciples got into a boat, and he said, "Let's cross the lake." They started out, [23] and while they were sailing across, he went to sleep.

Suddenly a strong wind struck the lake, and the boat started sinking. They were in danger. [24] So they went to Jesus and woke him up, "Master, Master! We are about to drown!"

Jesus got up and ordered the wind and waves to stop. They obeyed, and everything was calm. [25] Then Jesus asked the disciples, "Don't you have any faith?" But they were frightened and amazed. They said to each other, "Who is this? He can give orders to the wind and the waves, and they obey him!"

Continued overpage

When bad things happen (continued ...)

The disciples knew Jesus could help but they were upset when he stayed asleep. Then things happened!

What an amazing person!

Prayer: Jesus, when bad things happen to me, help me to remember that you are still there, caring for me.

pp nd
kn th
wh
th mp

See if you can complete this puzzle.
In the bag there are seven pairs of letters.
Choose which letters fit in the gaps.

It is i_ _ortant to
_ _ow _ _at Jesus
loves a_ _ cares
for me, even
_ _en bad _ _ings
ha_ _en.

Someone in a crowd

When Samuel returned to Hotshots Club he was a hero with his plaster cast and crutches. Everyone crowded around wanting to talk.

In today's Bible verses, a much bigger crowd kept trying to get to Jesus.

Luke 8:40-42

40 Everyone had been waiting for Jesus, and when he came back, a crowd was there to welcome him.

41 Just then the man in charge of the Jewish meeting place came and knelt down in front of Jesus. His name was Jairus, and he begged Jesus to come to his home 42 because his 12-year-old child was dying. She was his only daughter.

A surprising interruption – but keep reading.

Luke 8:49-53

49 While Jesus was speaking, someone came from Jairus' home and said, "Your daughter has died! Why bother the teacher any more?"

50 When Jesus heard this, he told Jairus, "Don't worry! Have faith, and your daughter will get well."

51 Jesus went into the house, but he did not let anyone else go with him, except Peter, John, James, and the girl's father and mother. 52 Everyone was crying and weeping for the girl. But Jesus said, "The child isn't dead. She is just asleep." 53 The people laughed at him because they knew she was dead.

Continued overpage

Someone in a crowd

(continued ...)

Luke 8:54-56

[54] Jesus took hold of the girl's hand and said, "Child, get up!" [55] She came back to life and got right up. Jesus told them to give her something to eat. [56] Her parents were surprised, but Jesus ordered them not to tell anyone what had happened.

Jairus was an important person. He was very worried about his daughter. When Jesus was interrupted on his way to the girl, Jairus must have been annoyed and anxious.

Look at verse 56. Why do you think Jesus told her parents to keep it a secret?

☐ He didn't want people to gossip.

☐ He didn't want people to stare at her.

☐ Or, write your own answer

Prayer: Thank you Jesus that you know what is best. I can trust you to care for me.

Hotshots training session

Catching and throwing

1. Hold the ball close to your chest, so you don't get bumped and drop the ball.

2. Spread your hands around the ball. Keep your fingers relaxed but not floppy.

3. Throw from your chest towards your friend's chest. Aim for their jumper or shirt.

4. When you throw flick your hands with a snap.

5. Keep practising!

Jesus interrupted on his way

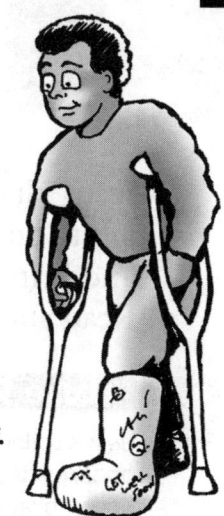

With his plaster cast, Samuel felt important. But he remembered how embarrassed and scared he was when he fell over and broke his leg.

What happened to Jesus on his way to the home of Chairman Jairus?

Luke 8:43-48

43 In the crowd was a woman who had been bleeding for 12 years. She had spent everything she had on doctors, but none of them could make her well.

44 As soon as she came up behind Jesus and barely touched his clothes, her bleeding stopped.

45 "Who touched me?" Jesus asked.

While everyone was denying it, Peter said, "Master, people are crowding all around and pushing you from every side."

46 But Jesus answered, "Someone touched me, because I felt power going out from me." 47 The woman knew that she couldn't hide, so she came trembling and knelt down in front of Jesus. She told everyone why she had touched him and that she had been healed straight away.

48 Jesus said to the woman, "You're now well because of your faith. May God give you peace!"

What a surprise! The woman was too shy to speak to Jesus so she tried to get his help secretly. She was so embarrassed about her illness and couldn't go out often or live a normal life.

Jesus encouraged her not to hide her secret. This was hard to do, but Jesus knew it was best for her. Now everyone knew she was well again. She could live a normal life and be with her family and friends.

Prayer: *Lord Jesus, sometimes I have to do hard things when I don't want to. Please help me to do them.*

Learn by doing

Jesus' disciples had a similar job to do – making friends and bringing them along. Read about it.

Luke 9:1-6

[1] Jesus called together his twelve apostles and gave them complete power over all demons and diseases. [2] Then he sent them to tell about God's kingdom and to heal the sick. [3] He told them, "Don't take anything with you! Don't take a walking stick or a travelling bag or food or money or even a change of clothes. [4] When you are welcomed into a home, stay there until you leave that town. [5] If people won't welcome you, leave the town and shake the dust from your feet as a warning to them." [6] The apostles left and went from village to village, telling the good news and healing people everywhere.

Draw a circle around the things that Jesus told the disciples NOT to take.

Walking stick,   sandals,   clothes,

hat,   food,   money,

travel bag,   change of clothes.

Think why Jesus might have said this? Tick any box that matches your ideas.

☐ They were learning to trust God for their needs.

☐ They were learning to trust other people for their needs.

☐ He wanted them to live as poor people.

Prayer: *Help me to do a good job as a member of your team.*

> Next week we'll have a 'bring a friend' night. Maybe you can each bring a friend to Hotshots.

Picnic time

Emily was cooking pancakes for the Hotshots Club. Suddenly lots of new kids arrived. She didn't have enough and the shops were shut already. How would you feel if this happened to you? Annoyed? Embarrassed? Excited? Puzzled?

Jesus had a similar experience.

Luke 9:10-17

[10] The apostles came back and told Jesus everything they had done. He then took them with him to the village of Bethsaida, where they could be alone. [11] But a lot of people found out about this and followed him. Jesus welcomed them. He spoke to them about God's kingdom and healed everyone who was sick.

[12] Late in the afternoon the twelve apostles came to Jesus and said, "Send the crowd to the villages and farms around here. They need to find a place to stay and something to eat. There is nothing in this place. It's like a desert!"

[13] Jesus answered, "You give them something to eat."

But they replied, "We have only five small loaves of bread and two fish. If we are going to feed all these people, we will have to go and buy food." [14] There were about 5000 men in the crowd.

Jesus said to his disciples, "Have the people sit in groups of 50." [15] They did this, and all the people sat down. [16] Jesus took the five loaves and the two fish. He looked up towards heaven and blessed the food. Then he broke the bread and fish and handed them to his disciples to give to the people.

[17] Everyone ate all they wanted. What was left over filled 12 baskets.

Continued overpage

Picnic time
(continued ...)

Jesus told the people to sit down for a meal. The disciples may have got angry with Jesus. Perhaps they thought they would soon look stupid.

Prayer: *Thank you that you still care about the many hungry people in the world. Please help me to share what I have.*

These words are in the wrong order. Start with the last word and copy them in the correct order.

Everyone for cares and loves He.
Amazing is Jesus.

_____

_____

To do: Ask your parents to contact groups like Tear Fund or World Vision to find out ways you can help people who are hungry.

What's next?

When you have finished this *Hotshots*, go for others in the series.

Other books include:

- *Mini stars of the Bible*
  Find out about Bible kids and their families

- *Growing as a follower of Jesus*
  Find out what Jesus taught about the way to live

- *Sticking close to God*
  Find out how to pray

- *Time-ship to Bible-land*
  Find out about life in Bible times

An important question

Hong had an important question to ask his Mum. He got a camera for his birthday and films cost a lot! Now he's short of money. 'I wonder if Mum will give me money for a film. She's busy now – I'll ask her later.' Jesus had an important question to ask his disciples. He waited for a good time.

Luke 9:18-21

18 When Jesus was alone praying, his disciples came to him, and he asked them, "What do people say about me?"

19 They answered, "Some say that you are John the Baptist or Elijah or a prophet from long ago who has come back to life."

20 Jesus then asked them, "But who do you say I am?" Peter answered, "You are the Messiah sent from God."

21 Jesus strictly warned his disciples not to tell anyone about this.

Can you spot the really important question? It's in verse 20.

Peter knew the answer. The 'Messiah' was a Champion Leader or King promised by God. Much more special than John, or Elijah or anyone else!

Prayer: Thank you for sending Jesus to be a Champion Leader. Help me to understand how special he is.

24 Not an easy life

Luke 9:22-25

22 Jesus told his disciples, "The nation's leaders, the chief priests, and the teachers of the Law of Moses will make the Son of Man suffer terribly. They will reject him and kill him, but three days later he will rise to life."

23 Then Jesus said to all the people: "If any of you want to be my followers, you must forget about yourself. You must take up your cross each day and follow me. 24 If you want to save your life, you will destroy it. But if you give up your life for me, you will save it. 25 What will you gain, if you own the whole world but destroy yourself or waste your life?

> Following Jesus is exciting and special, but sometimes it can be tough. Things were very tough for Jesus.

Think carefully about these verses, then write T (true) or F (false) next to each of these statements.

Following Jesus…

☐ makes you feel holy and religious all the time

☐ can be as hard as carrying a heavy wooden cross

☐ can be embarrassing

☐ makes you feel happy all the time.
Answers below.

Look again at verse 23. Have you made up your mind to be a follower of Jesus too? If you want to know how, see page 95.

Prayer: Please help me to understand how to be a follower of Jesus.

> What do the Hotshot team members think of Jesus?

> I think I would like to follow Jesus always!

> I'm not sure what I think.

True/False answers: F, T, T, F

An amazing experience

One morning, very early, Jeff took the Hotshots to a beach for breakfast.

Jesus took his best friends up a mountain. What they saw was so amazing they could hardly believe it.

I like the sunrise and the early morning. It was so good. I just want to be quiet.

Luke 9:28-36

28 About eight days later Jesus took Peter, John, and James with him and went up on a mountain to pray. 29 While he was praying, his face changed, and his clothes became shining white. 30 Suddenly Moses and Elijah were there speaking with him. 31 They appeared in heavenly glory and talked about all that Jesus' death in Jerusalem would mean.

32 Peter and the other two disciples had been sound asleep. All at once they woke up and saw how glorious Jesus was. They also saw the two men who were with him.

33 Moses and Elijah were about to leave, when Peter said to Jesus, "Master, it's good for us to be here! Let's make three shelters, one for you, one for Moses, and one for Elijah." But Peter didn't know what he was talking about.

34 While Peter was still speaking, a shadow from a cloud passed over them, and they were frightened as the cloud covered them. 35 From the cloud a voice spoke, "This is my chosen Son. Listen to what he says!" 36 After the voice had spoken, Peter, John, and James saw only Jesus. For some time they kept quiet and did not say anything about what they had seen.

Continued overpage

An amazing experience
(continued ...)

Look again at verse 31. See what Jesus, Moses and Elijah were talking about.

Why was this happening so special? (Look at verse 35.) Because Jesus was there.

God said 'Listen to Jesus.' How do we do this? Here are four ways.

1. We read the Bible.
2. Older Christians teach us.
3. We do what our parents tell us.
4. Sometimes deep inside, we get a feeling that we know what is right.

In the first picture frame, draw a picture of the special time in this story. In the second picture frame draw yourself close to Jesus. Write what you would talk about.

Prayer: Thank you God for the special times when I feel you are really close.

26 Everybody's welcome

Jesus' followers argued about who was best. They were not encouraging each other like the Hotshots.

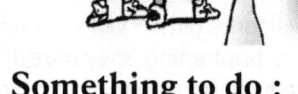

Don't stop. You're getting better each time we play!

I think I'll leave Hotshots. It's hard to play basketball. I'm not as good as Samuel is. And I'm only short!

Luke 9:46-48

46 Jesus' disciples were arguing about which one of them was the greatest. 47 Jesus knew what they were thinking, and he had a child stand there beside him. 48 Then he said to his disciples, "When you welcome even a child because of me, you welcome me. And when you welcome me, you welcome the one who sent me. Whichever one of you is the most humble is the greatest."

Even if you don't feel special, Jesus says you are. Jesus doesn't push you away. You are welcome, sometimes more welcome than adults!

Prayer: *I'm glad you welcome me. Help me to remember this when other people ignore me and put me down.*

I'm Special! Jesus said so!

Something to do :

Cut a circle out of card – about 10 cm across. On it print the words: 'I'm special! Jesus said so!' Thread some wool or string and hang it on your bed or your window.

Not welcome

There was one place where Jesus was not made welcome and his followers became angry.

Luke 9:51-55

51 Not long before it was time for Jesus to be taken up to heaven, he made up his mind to go to Jerusalem. 52 He sent some messengers on ahead to a Samaritan village to get things ready for him. 53 But he was on his way to Jerusalem, so the people there refused to welcome him. 54 When the disciples James and John saw what was happening, they asked, "Lord, do you want us to call down fire from heaven to destroy these people?" 55 But Jesus turned and corrected them for what they had said.

James and John said something like this: 'They can't do that to us. We're with Jesus and we're special. Let's pay them back. Jesus has the power to zap them. That will teach them a lesson.'

Some kids at school said they want to join Hotshots, but I told them there was no more room in the team.

I think it's important to try to make them feel welcome.

Was Jesus pleased that they were so bossy? (See verse 55)

Prayer: Lord Jesus, please help me learn that paying back is not your way.

28 More followers

Jesus had many more friends than his famous twelve disciples. Here are another seventy.

Luke 10:1,2,5,6,8,9

[1]Later the Lord chose 72 other followers and sent them out two by two to every town and village where he was about to go. [2]He said to them: 'A large crop is in the fields, but there are only a few workers. Ask the Lord in charge of the harvest to send out workers to bring it in.

[5]As soon as you enter a home, say, "God bless this home with peace." [6]If the people living there are peace-loving, your prayer for peace will bless them. But if they are not peace-loving, your prayer will return to you.

[8]If the people of a town welcome you, eat whatever they offer. [9]Heal their sick and say, "God's kingdom will soon be here!"'

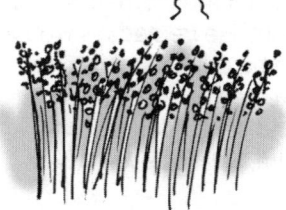

Jesus said, 'People are like crops on a farm. Let's be farmers and try to harvest them!'

Think of someone you know who is not a follower of Jesus. Pray for them.

Prayer: *Lord Jesus, please help _____ [include the name of your friend here] discover how wonderful you are.*

Be a caring person

Emily said she thought she wasn't good at basketball, but since then, Samuel has been practising with her. They've been shooting baskets together after school.

One day a man came to Jesus to find out how to serve God better. Jesus told him a story, that is now famous, about a man caring for a stranger in trouble.

Luke 10:30-35

[30] Jesus replied: As a man was going down from Jerusalem to Jericho, robbers attacked him and grabbed everything he had. They beat him up and ran off, leaving him half dead.

[31] A priest happened to be going down the same road. But when he saw the man, he walked by on the other side. [32] Later a temple helper came to the same place. But when he saw the man who had been beaten up, he also went by on the other side.

[33] A man from Samaria then came travelling along that road. When he saw the man, he felt sorry for him [34] and went over to him. He treated his wounds with olive oil and wine and bandaged them. Then he put him on his own donkey and took him to an inn, where he took care of him. [35] The next morning he gave the innkeeper two silver coins and said, "Please take care of the man. If you spend more than this on him, I will pay you when I return."

Luke 10:36-37

36 Then Jesus asked, "Which one of these three people was a real neighbor to the man who was beaten up by robbers?" 37 The teacher answered, "The one who showed pity." Jesus said, "Go and do the same!"

A secret plan:

Think of something caring that you could do as a surprise for someone you know. Keep it a secret. When they least expect it, surprise them. Don't look for thanks or praise.

Prayer: *Please help me with my secret plan. And don't let me get too proud about it please!*

Hotshots training session

Send a bounce throw

Same as throwing, but this time you aim for the floor between you and your friend. Then the ball bounces up to meet your friend about as high as their shorts.

Remember, keep your eyes open and aim for your friend.
Be alert.

Keep trying till you feel better about your throwing.

30

Food or friendship?

Emily's basketball skills were improving fast. She was determined to become the team's best player.

When Jeff called the team together to read the Bible and pray, Emily groaned and stamped her feet. 'I need to keep practising', she shouted, 'I haven't got time for that Bible stuff!'

This reminded Jeff about two friends of Jesus – Mary and Martha.

Luke 10:38-42

38 The Lord and his disciples were travelling along and came to a village. When they got there, a woman named Martha welcomed him into her home. 39 She had a sister named Mary, who sat down in front of the Lord and was listening to what he said. 40 Martha was worried about all that had to be done. Finally, she went to Jesus and said, "Lord, doesn't it bother you that my sister has left me to do all the work by myself? Tell her to come and help me!"

41 The Lord answered, "Martha, Martha! You are worried and upset about so many things, 42 but only one thing is necessary. Mary has chosen what is best, and it will not be taken away from her."

Jesus loved going to people's homes and sharing meals with them. It was the **people** not the **food** that mattered to him!

These sisters were very different.

Compare them:

Drawing lines to join the circles with the correct squares

Mary wanted to

   be sure that ❑

○ she served everything perfectly even though it took a lot of time.

Martha wanted to

   be sure that ❑

○ she listened to Jesus and spent time with him.

Prayer: *Dear God, please teach me how to pray and help me with my Hotshots Bible readings.*

Here is a difficult code puzzle – can you do it?
First you need the code.

Code: a = 1, e = 2, i = 3, o = 4 and u = 5

W2 n22d t4 m1k2 t3m2 t4 t1lk 1nd l3st2n t4 J2s5s.

_____

_____

_____

Your Hotshots readings are a way of listening to Jesus. When you have finished them each day, you could take a couple of minutes to pray. There are some good tips about this on pages 48 and 49.

Time-out

'Go! Jeff! Go!', the Hotshots shouted. They were watching Jeff play for his team. Dan asked Jeff after, 'What did the coach say during Time-out?' 'He told us what we were doing wrong and how to play better,' Jeff explained. 'He drew game diagrams to make it clear. We listen and do what he says – even if we don't like his ideas.'

Jesus needed to take 'Time-out' too. He went away often to spend time alone with God.

Luke 11:1-4

[1]When Jesus had finished praying, one of his disciples said to him, "Lord, teach us to pray, just as John taught his followers to pray." [2] So Jesus told them, "Pray in this way:
  'Father, help us to honour your name.
  Come and set up your kingdom.
  [3] Give us each day the food we need.
  [4] Forgive our sins, as we forgive everyone who has
    done wrong to us.
  And keep us from being tempted.' "

'Why pray?' Dan asks. ' God knows everything already.'

'God is our loving Father. He wants us to tell him what's on our mind', Jeff says. He wants us to listen also when we pray. Sometimes he puts good ideas in our minds. God is everywhere. He is never too busy to hear us. Talk to him anytime, but a special **Time-out** each day is helpful.'

Prayer: *Dear God, please help me to practise listening to you when I pray.*

32

God is listening for you

MR MEAN

MR HAPPY

MR GRUMPY

When you were little, did you read any 'Mr Men' books?
What did Mr Happy look like? Mr Grumpy?
Mr Mean? Draw them in this frame. (If you can't
remember the Mr Men people, make up your own.)

Jesus made up a story about two men.
We'll call them Mr Friendly and Mr Grumpy.

Luke 11:9-13

⁹ So I tell you to ask and you will receive, search and you will find, knock and the door will be opened for you. ¹⁰ Everyone who asks will receive, everyone who searches will find, and the door will be opened for everyone who knocks. ¹¹ Which one of you fathers would give your hungry child a snake if the child asked for a fish? ¹² Which one of you would give your child a scorpion if the child asked for an egg? ¹³ As bad as you are, you still know how to give good gifts to your children. But your heavenly Father is even more ready to give the Holy Spirit to anyone who asks.'

If even mean and grumpy people listen to you, we can expect our kind heavenly Father to listen to what we say.

So never be too embarrassed or shy to tell God how you really feel!

Prayer: *Dear God, when I have 'Time-out' with you, help me to remember that you are really listening and caring.*

Time-out with God

The Hotshots prayer list

Keeping a list of things you talk about with God, will help you not to be selfish. Here is the Hotshots prayer list. You might like to add some extra things that are very special to you. Or you might like to list people who are often on your mind.

Sunday

A good day to pray for **your church**. Pray for your minister or your Club leader or your Sunday School teacher.

_____

_____

Monday

The first day of **school** for the week. Pray for your teacher and for your school friends.

_____

_____

Tuesday

Pray for members of your **family** at home.

_____

_____

_____

Wednesday

Pray about the things that you need **help** with – maybe wrong habits or things you find hard to do.

_____

_____

Time-out with God

Thursday

Pray about **people who are really ill** – the disabled, the very old, or those sick with a disease. Especially pray for

_____

_____ (write the name.)

Friday

Pray about the **sad things** you see on the TV news – people without food or the really poor. Pray for those who help them.

_____

_____

Saturday

A day to relax. Pray for your **best friends**. Pray for help to be a good friend to them. Pray especially for

_____

_____ (write the name.)

A voice in the crowd

The Hotshots were watching Jeff play his match in the top basketball competition. It was so exciting! When the scores were levelled, one very loud voice was heard above the cheers of the crowd. 'You're a star, Jeff!' Everyone heard him. The team's cheer squad started up. Soon everyone was screaming and cheering. Jeff scored a slam dunk – what a star!

One day someone called out a similar thing to Jesus.

You're a star, Jeff!

'Wouldn't it be great to be Jesus' mum', said the woman. Jesus was probably pleased because, to him, his mother was a very special person. But Jesus wanted to say something more. 'My mum is certainly very special, but I have news for you. Everyone who lives for God is special too.'

What is so special is that Jesus probably has the biggest family in the world! Anyone can join. To find out more about being part of Jesus' family, turn to page 95.

We belong to Jesus' family.

Luke 11:27-28

[27] While Jesus was still talking, a woman in the crowd spoke up, "The woman who gave birth to you and fed you is blessed!" [28] Jesus replied, "That's true, but the people who are really blessed are the ones who hear and obey God's message!"

Prayer: Dear Jesus, thank you for welcoming us and making us part of your family. Please help me to understand what this means.

turn to page 95.

34

Taking notice

The Hotshots went to see Jeff play a match with the 'Bullets'. They noticed how **tall** the Bullets team were! They noticed something else. Some of the Bullets were really happy to chat with them and give them basketball tips. But some of the team didn't take any notice of the Hotshots because they were only kids.

Luke 18:15-17

15 Some people brought their little children for Jesus to bless. But when his disciples saw them doing this, they told the people to stop bothering him.

16 So Jesus called the children over to him and said, "Let the children come to me! Don't try to stop them. People who are like these children belong to God's kingdom. 17 You will never get into God's kingdom unless you enter it like a child!"

Do you know how tall you are?

Write it here _____.

If you don't know, find a tape or long ruler and measure yourself. A special thing about Jesus was that he noticed people who were small or unimportant. Can you remember another story about him helping someone that others ignored?

Prayer: Dear Lord Jesus, I'm glad you think I am special because I usually feel unimportant.

35

The best gear

Hong arrived at Hotshots wearing a brand new tracksuit and basketball cap. Chris grew quiet. Jeff noticed that Chris was not joking as much as usual and asked why. 'Nothing' said Chris, but saying under his breath, 'Why am I always the one who has to wear second-hand stuff and hand-me-downs!'

Jeff chose this reading to show what Jesus had to say about things that are really important.

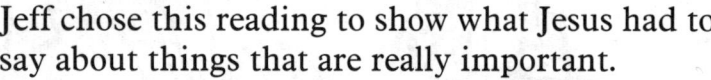

Luke 12:22-31

[22] Jesus said to his disciples: "I tell you not to worry about your life! Don't worry about having something to eat or wear. [23] Life is more than food or clothing. [25] Can worry make you live longer? [26] If you don't have power over small things, why worry about everything else?

[27] Look how the wild flowers grow! They don't work hard to make their clothes. But I tell you that Solomon with all his wealth wasn't as well clothed as one of these flowers. [28] God gives such beauty to everything that grows in the fields, even though it is here today and thrown into a fire tomorrow. Won't he do even more for you? You have such little faith!

[29] Don't keep worrying about having something to eat or drink. [30] Only people who don't know God are always worrying about such things. Your Father knows what you need. [31] But put God's work first, and these things will be yours as well."

Think carefully about what Jesus said. Write in the speech bubble what you would say to Chris.

Prayer: Dear God, I know I have to be careful about my things and thankful for what I've got. But please help me not to be envious or to get annoyed about what others have.

36 Bad luck happens

Some of the Hotshots remembered when Samuel broke his leg. Kim asked, 'How come bad luck happens?' Jeff explained, 'Some bad things happen because bad people cause them. Mostly bad things are accidents or just happen. We don't know why. It's a mystery. But it's worth finding out what Jesus thinks.'

Luke 13:1-5

[1]About this same time Jesus was told that Pilate had given orders for some people from Galilee to be killed while they were offering sacrifices. [2]Jesus replied: "Do you think that these people were worse sinners than everyone else in Galilee just because of what happened to them? [3]Not at all! But you can be sure that if you don't turn back to God, every one of you will also be killed. [4]What about those 18 people who died when the tower in Siloam fell on them? Do you think they were worse than everyone else in Jerusalem? [5]Not at all! But you can be sure that if you don't turn back to God, every one of you will also die."

Bad luck usually happens when you don't expect it. It happens whether you've been bad or good. But Jesus explains one important thing…

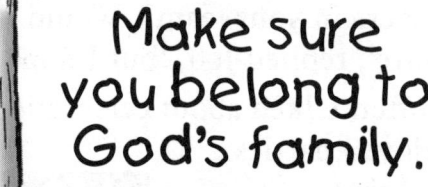

Make sure you belong to God's family.

God can help us cope when bad things happen.

Prayer: *Dear God, whatever happens, please help me to remember that you are there – always.*

Remember: To think about being part of Jesus' family, turn to page 94 and 95.

The greatest party of all!

The Hotshots were planing the end of season celebration party. 'Who should we invite?', asked Jeff. 'Then we should decide what we will do and what to eat.'

Samuel said to Jeff, 'Can we invite some of the ace players in your team? Would they come?' 'Not sure', replied Jeff, 'but I hope so.'

Jesus often talked about celebrations. He enjoyed parties. He said that when we say, 'Yes' to joining his family, it is just like saying 'Yes' to an invitation to a party.

Luke 14:15-21

[15] After Jesus had finished speaking, one of the guests said, "The greatest blessing of all is to be at the banquet in God's kingdom!"

[16] Jesus told him: 'A man once gave a great banquet and invited a lot of guests. [17] When the banquet was ready, he sent a servant to tell the guests, "Everything is ready! Please come." [18] One guest after another started making excuses. The first one said, "I bought some land, and I've got to look it over. Please excuse me." [19] Another guest said, "I bought five teams of oxen, and I need to try them out. Please excuse me." [20] Still another guest said, "I've just got married, and I can't be there." [21] The servant told his master what happened, and the master became so angry that he said, "Go as fast as you can to every street and alley in town! Bring in everyone who is poor or crippled or blind or lame."

Think about the replies given by the people who were invited. What do you think of them? (Tick one or two answers)

☐ Not very polite

☐ Truthful and honest

☐ Rude

☐ Made-up excuses.

Jesus was angry that some people refused his invitation to join his family. So he asked those he knew would like to come.

Prayer: *Lord Jesus, thank you for inviting me to join your family. Please help me to think carefully about this.*

The missing letters for the code message are in the party balloons. Write the correct letters to make the message complete.

__od __s __ery

__appy __hen __e

__ay __es __o __im.

God comes looking

One night at Hotshots, Hong got very upset about something Dan said. He marched out and slammed the door angrily and didn't come back in. Everyone was puzzled. It made them sad. Kim went outside looking for Hong. Soon she came back with Hong. He still looked hurt and disappointed but Kim's care helped.

Jesus told some made-up stories to show how God takes the trouble to find people who are alone. He encourages them to come to him.

Luke 15:4-7

4 'If any of you has a 100 sheep, and one of them gets lost, what will you do? Won't you leave the 99 in the field and go look for the lost sheep until you find it? 5 And when you find it, you will be so glad that you will put it on your shoulder 6 and carry it home. Then you will call in your friends and neighbors and say, "Let's celebrate! I've found my lost sheep."

7 Jesus said, "In the same way there is more happiness in heaven because of one sinner who turns to God than over 99 good people who don't need to."

These words describe how the farmer and the lost sheep felt when the sheep was found. Use a blue pen to circle words for the farmer, and a red pen for the sheep.

relieved   safe   angry

happy   tired

disappointed   proud   pleased

When Hong came back inside, Dan said he was sorry. Kim was pleased that she helped and Dan and Hong were pleased to be friends again. All the Hotshots were happy again. God too is happy when people get to know him as a friend.

Luke 15:8-10

8 Jesus told the people another story: 'What will a woman do if she has ten silver coins and loses one of them? Won't she light a lamp, sweep the floor, and look carefully until she finds it? 9 Then she will call in her friends and neighbours and say, "Let's celebrate! I've found the coin I lost." ' 10 Jesus said, "In the same way God's angels are happy when even one person turns to him."

What is the most valuable thing you own?

How would you feel if you lost it or broke it?

God feels like that when people ignore him.

Prayer: Dear God, thanks again for going to lots of trouble to care for me.

Still Looking!

After Hong came back, the Hotshots played basketball better. They seemed to have more teamwork, more energy, now the quarrel was over.

Jeff encouraged everyone to listen to another one of Jesus' stories about a family having troubles and a father who cared.

Luke 15:11-24

[11] Jesus also told them another story: 'Once a man had two sons. [12] The younger son said to his father, "Give me my share of the property." So the father divided his property between his two sons.

[13] Not long after that, the younger son packed up everything he owned and left for a foreign country, where he wasted all his money in wild living. [14] He had spent everything, when a bad famine spread through that whole land. Soon he had nothing to eat.

[15] He went to work for a man in that country, and the man sent him out to take care of his pigs. [16] He would have been glad to eat what the pigs were eating, but no one gave him a thing.

[17] Finally, he came to his senses and said, "My father's workers have plenty to eat, and here I am, starving to death! [18] I will go to my father and say to him, 'Father, I've sinned against God in heaven and against you. [19] I'm no longer good enough to be called your son. Treat me like one of your workers.' "

[20] The younger son got up and started back to his father. But when he was still a long way off, his father saw him and felt sorry for him. He ran to his son and hugged and kissed him.

²¹ The son said, "Father, I've sinned against God in heaven and against you. I'm no longer good enough to be called your son."

²² But his father said to the servants, "Hurry and bring the best clothes and put them on him. Give him a ring for his finger and sandals for his feet. ²³ Get the best calf and prepare it, so we can eat and celebrate. ²⁴ This son of mine was dead, but has now come back to life. He was lost and has now been found." And they began to celebrate.

Notice the three main people in this story – the father, the young son and the older son. Remember the 'Mr Men' characters on page 42? Do any of these 'Mr Men' names fit our story? If not think of some names of your own. Then draw a 'Mr Men' person in each picture frame.

MR MEAN

MR GREEDY

MR JELLY

MR BOUNCE

MR HAPPY

MR TICKLE

MR SILLY

MR GRUMPY

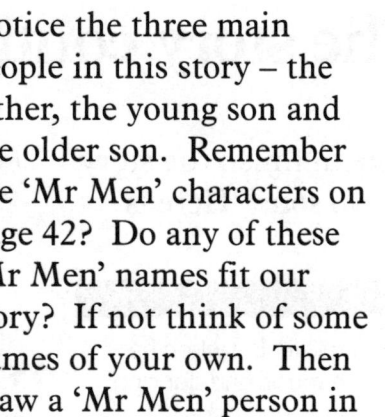

Father   *Young Son*   *Older Son*

You could call the father Mr God (because that is his real name in the story!) Because Mr God is a spirit without a human body, you won't be able to draw him!

Continued overpage

EXTRA! The story continues

We thought you may like to finish the story about the man and his two sons. Here is the rest of it.

Luke 15:25-32

25 The older son had been out in the field. But when he came near the house, he heard the music and dancing. 26 So he called one of the servants over and asked, "What's going on here?"

27 The servant answered, "Your brother has come home safe and sound, and your father ordered us to kill the best calf." 28 The older brother got so angry that he would not even go into the house. His father came out and begged him to go in. 29 But he said to his father, "For years I have worked for you like a slave and have always obeyed you. But you have never even given me a little goat, so that I could give a dinner for my friends. 30 This other son of yours wasted your money on prostitutes. And now that he has come home, you ordered the best calf to be killed for a feast." '

31 His father replied, "My son, you're always with me, and everything I have is yours. 32 But we should be glad and celebrate! Your brother was dead, but he is now alive. He was lost and has now been found."

Prayer: *Thank you dear God, for loving me like a very strong and caring father. Please help me not to leave you or be mean when other people love you.*

Check: There is more about how to be part of God's family on pages 94 and 95.

Find Out

In the next Hotshots reading we will find out about a man who had a terrible skin disease. In Bible times all skin diseases like 'leprosy' were thought to be catching. People with leprosy kept away from others. (With real leprosy people lose feeling in their hands and feet. It can cause terrible injuries.) Your parents can help you contact The Leprosy Mission to find out more.

Thank you!

At the next practice, Hong shared a big bag of potato chips. Everyone was eager to have some when the bag was passed around. Jeff wondered whether this was Hong's way of saying 'Sorry' and 'Thank you' after the quarrel. No one asked about it, but everyone enjoyed crunching the chips. People rarely say 'thank you'. That's sad. Here's something that happened with Jesus.

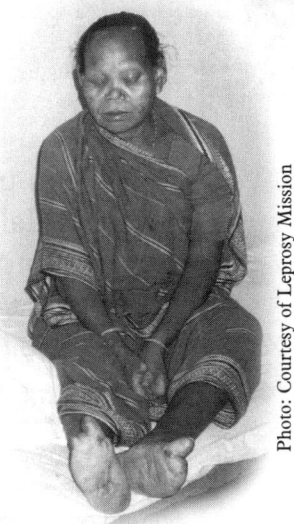

Photo: Courtesy of Leprosy Mission

Luke 17:11-19

[11] On his way to Jerusalem, Jesus went along the border between Samaria and Galilee. [12] As he was going into a village, ten men with leprosy came towards him. They stood at a distance [13] and shouted, "Jesus, Master, have pity on us!"

[14] Jesus looked at them and said, "Go show yourselves to the priests." On their way they were healed. [15] When one of them discovered that he was healed, he came back, shouting praises to God. [16] He bowed down at the feet of Jesus and thanked him. The man was from the country of Samaria. [17] Jesus asked, "Weren't ten men healed? Where are the other nine? [18] Why was this foreigner the only one who came back to thank God?" [19] Then Jesus told the man, "You may get up and go. Your faith has made you well."

You can find out a little more about leprosy on page 60 (opposite).

Prayer: *Dear God, please help me to say thank you for things I receive – especially to you, and to my family.*

42

Hearing and seeing

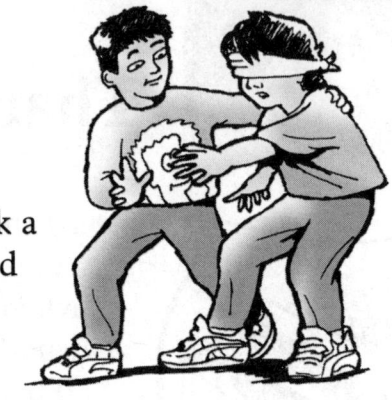

To learn to trust each other in the team, the Hotshots each took a partner. Half of them put on blindfolds. Their partners guided them around the court. It was fun. They knew they would be able to see again when the blindfolds came off! Imagine what it would be like to be blind all the time.

Luke 18:35-43

[35] When Jesus was coming close to Jericho, a blind man sat begging beside the road. [36] The man heard the crowd walking by and asked what was happening. [37] Some people told him that Jesus from Nazareth was passing by. [38] So the blind man shouted, "Jesus, Son of David, have pity on me!" [39] The people who were going along with Jesus told the man to be quiet. But he shouted even louder, "Son of David, have pity on me!"

[40] Jesus stopped and told some people to bring the blind man over to him. When the blind man was getting near, Jesus asked, [41] "What do you want me to do for you?" "Lord, I want to see!" he answered.

[42] Jesus replied, "Look and you will see! Your eyes are healed because of your faith." [43] Straight away the man could see, and he went with Jesus and started thanking God. When the crowds saw what happened, they praised God.

Write one word (or draw his face) to say how the man felt in these verses.

Verse 36 _____

Verse 39 _____

Verse 40 _____

Verse 43 _____

What was the first thing he saw?

_____

What do you think he noticed?

_____

Prayer: Please Jesus, help me to keep following you no matter what other people say.

A new way to live

Some of you are forgetting our team work.

Things were serious. When the Hotshots met, Jeff asked everyone to gather round. "We are forgetting our team work. You are playing selfishly and not looking out for each other. You are even forgetting some basic rules. Let's play like a new team. Listen to me, then you won't go wrong."

A man called Zac had to learn a new way of living. The change was amazing.

Luke 19:1-9

¹Jesus was going through Jericho, ²where a man named Zacchaeus lived. He was in charge of collecting taxes and was very rich. ³⁻⁴Jesus was heading his way, and Zacchaeus wanted to see what he was like. But Zacchaeus was a short man and couldn't see over the crowd. So he ran ahead and climbed up into a sycamore tree.

⁵When Jesus got there, he looked up and said, "Zacchaeus, hurry down! I want to stay with you today." ⁶Zacchaeus hurried down and gladly welcomed Jesus.

⁷Everyone who saw this started grumbling, "This man Zacchaeus is a sinner! And Jesus is going home to eat with him."

⁸Later that day Zacchaeus stood up and said to the Lord, "I'll give half of my property to the poor. And I'll now pay back four times as much to everyone I've ever cheated."

⁹Jesus said to Zacchaeus, "Today you and your family have been saved.

What a change! Look at this 'Before' and 'After' list. How did things change for Zac? (Well, some things!) Draw lines to connect the matching words.

Before	After
No friends	Honest
Short	Caring
Cheat	New friends
Selfish	Short

Prayer: Lord Jesus, you are interested in all kinds of people. Thanks that you want me to be your friend.

Victory Lap

To encourage the Hotshots Jeff showed them some photos of the Bullets when they won the Grand Final. One showed the team celebrating, with the captain on their shoulders. In Bible times the people celebrated important victories. The winner rode through the city and the people put their clothes on the ground for him. This happened to Jesus when the people thought he was their favourite leader.

Luke 19:28-38

28 When Jesus had finished saying all this, he went on towards Jerusalem. 29 As he was getting near Bethphage and Bethany on the Mount of Olives, he sent two of his disciples on ahead. 30 He told them, "Go into the next village, where you will find a young donkey that has never been ridden. Untie the donkey and bring it here. 31 If anyone asks why you are doing that, just say, 'The Lord needs it.' "

32 They went off and found everything just as Jesus had said. 33 While they were untying the donkey, its owners asked, "Why are you doing that?" 34 They answered, "The Lord needs it."

35 Then they led the donkey to Jesus. They put some of their clothes on its back and helped Jesus get on. 36 And as he rode along, the people spread clothes on the road in front of him.

37 When Jesus was starting down the Mount of Olives, his large crowd of disciples were happy and praised God because of all the miracles they had seen. 38 They shouted, "Blessed is the king who comes in the name of the Lord! Peace in heaven and glory to God."

Notice what the people shouted:

Jesus is our king!

Hurray for our king!

He is the king that God sent us!

A king coming for war would normally ride a war-horse (These days it would be a tank or an armoured troop carrier.)

What did Jesus ride?

_____ .

This was a sign of peace. These animals are too slow and gentle for fighting!

Prayer: *Lord Jesus, I know that you want people to work together and not to fight each other. Please help me to live like this too.*

Hotshots training session

Warming up & cooling down

Whether you play basketball, football or any other sport, it is good to know about warming up and cooling down.

Before : warm up

Before a match or a training session take a few minutes to warm up:

- your body will get warm and ready to play
- your mind will be sharp and ready
- you have less chance of being injured
- and it's fun!

Turn to page 73 for more tips about warming up.

Watch out!

Jeff continued his serious coaching talk to encourage the Hotshots. Two ace tips are (1) don't cheat the opposing team – keep to the rules, and (2) support each other with good teamwork.

Many leaders forgot these tips in the city of Jerusalem where Jesus was. The Temple church was huge – there was room for thousands. There were lots of shops in the entrance selling things to help people worship. Some shop keepers were cheats trying to make lots of money. Jesus was angry with them.

**1. Don't Cheat
2. Good Teamwork**

Luke 19:45-47

[45] When Jesus entered the temple, he started chasing out the people who were selling things. [46] He told them, "The Scriptures say, 'My house should be a place of worship.' But you have made it a place where robbers hide!"

[47] Each day, Jesus kept on teaching in the temple. So the chief priests, the teachers of the Law of Moses, and some other important people tried to have him killed.

The city leaders became suspicious about Jesus and angry about the way the ordinary folks loved him. Jesus had better watch out! (see verse 47).

Prayer: *Lord Jesus, when I'm tempted to cheat or to make life hard for someone else, please help me to remember your example.*

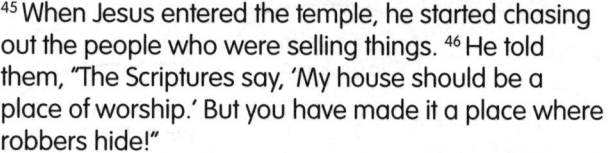

46

Give as much as you can!

'Time to clean up the hall today,' said Jeff. 'Let's do the work like we're playing a hard match. Give as much energy as you can – even if you run out of puff. Do your very, very best. Treat it like a game. You'll feel happy that you didn't give up!' Most were pleased to give a total effort.

Jesus noticed a person others ignored. The important people paid no attention to this very poor lady because they thought she didn't matter much to God. How wrong they were!

Luke 21:1-4

[1]Jesus looked up and saw some rich people tossing their gifts into the offering box. [2]He also saw a poor widow putting in two small coins. [3]And he said, "I tell you that this poor woman has put in more than all the others. [4]Everyone else gave what they didn't need. But she is very poor and gave everything she had."

Look at the lady's money sum... ...is worth more than ...

She had 0 left!

Prayer: Lord Jesus, please help me to be generous and unselfish to you and to others.

A dangerous trap for Jesus

The people in the city were glad to listen to Jesus. But the city leaders wanted Jesus stopped. They made their plans secretly. One day Mr X offered to tell them how to catch him. Who was the secret Mr X? Read and find out.

Luke 21:37-38, 22:1-6

37 Jesus taught in the temple each day, and he spent each night on the Mount of Olives. 38 Everyone got up early and came to the temple to hear him teach. The Festival of Thin Bread, also called Passover, was near. 2 The chief priests and the teachers of the Law of Moses were looking for a way to get rid of Jesus, because they were afraid of what the people might do. 3 Then Satan entered the heart of Judas Iscariot, who was one of the twelve apostles. 4 Judas went to talk with the chief priests and the officers of the temple police about how he could help them arrest Jesus. 5 They were very pleased and offered to pay Judas some money. 6 He agreed and started looking for a good chance to betray Jesus when the crowds were not around.

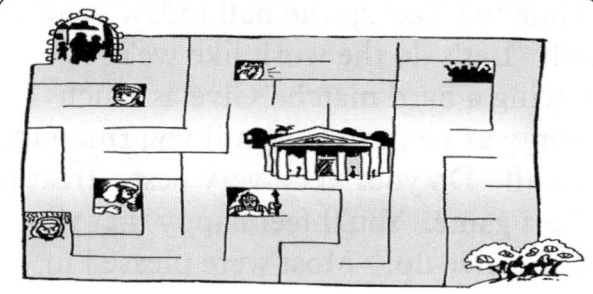

Draw a line to follow Jesus from the Mount of Olives to the Temple and back. Then draw a line for Judas from the City Gate to the Temple and back.

'How could anyone be an enemy of Jesus?', said Anna. 'It's hard to understand,' Jeff replied, 'but there are still enemies of Jesus right now. Be careful not to follow anyone who leads you away from Jesus.'

Prayer: Help me Lord Jesus, to be wise and to know who your real friends are.

A meal with Jesus

It was **Passover festival** time.

Meals were wonderful times with Jesus. He often taught and told stories at meals. This was Jesus' last meal with his friends before he died. He wanted them to keep on sharing meals, promising to still be with them in a new way.

Last Sunday we had Communion in our Church. What does it mean?

Let's read about how it began with Jesus.

Do you know?

Passover is the time when Jewish people remember how God rescued his people from being slaves in Egypt, 1300 years before Jesus was born. Bread and wine were always part of this meal.

Do you know?

Different churches have different names for this meal.
- Holy Communion
- Lord's Supper
- Eucharist

Continued overpage

A meal with Jesus (continued ...)

¹⁴ When the time came for Jesus and the apostles to eat.

¹⁷ Jesus took a cup of wine in his hands and gave thanks to God. Then he told the apostles, "Take this wine and share it with each other.
¹⁸ I tell you that I won't drink any more wine until God's kingdom comes."

¹⁹ Jesus took some bread in his hands and gave thanks for it. He broke the bread and handed it to his apostles. Then he said, "This is my body, which is given for you. Eat this as a way of remembering me!" ²⁰ After the meal he took another cup of wine in his hands. Then he said, "This is my blood. It is poured out for you, and with it God makes his new agreement.

What is the meaning of the Passover bread and wine? Jesus used these to show that he came to die to rescue us from our sin.

Draw strings to the matching tags to show what the meal meant.

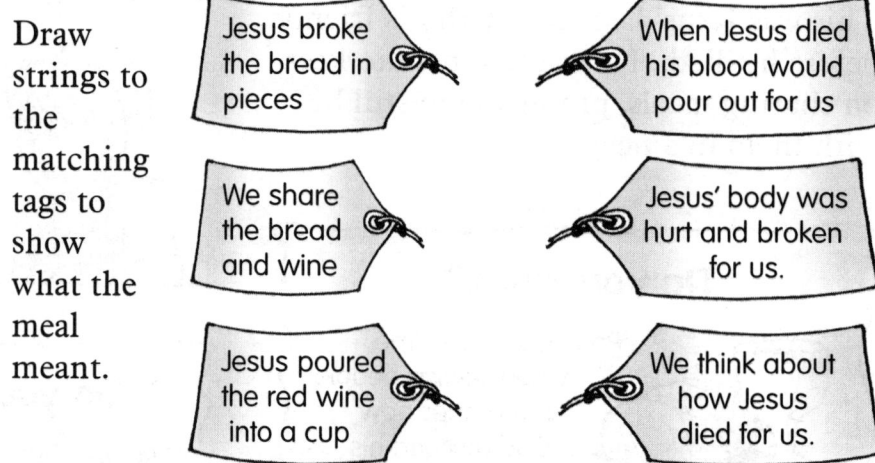

Jesus broke the bread in pieces

When Jesus died his blood would pour out for us

We share the bread and wine

Jesus' body was hurt and broken for us.

Jesus poured the red wine into a cup

We think about how Jesus died for us.

There is more about being part of God's family on page 94 and 95.

Prayer: *Thank you Lord Jesus that you died for me so that I can be forgiven and become part of your family.*

49 More quarrels

The Hotshots remembered the terrible time when Hong and Dan had a fight. Then it happened again! Chris thought he should be the team captain – he was the tallest and fastest. Anna thought she should be captain – she was better at shooting goals. Soon they were picking on and insulting each other.

Jeff put a stop to it. The captain should be the person who helps everyone play best.'
Read what Jesus said:

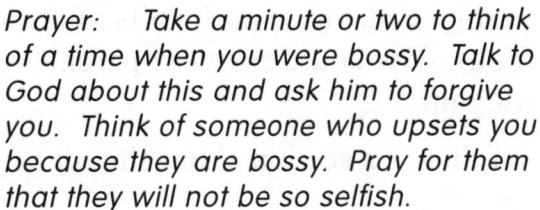

This kind of quarrelling wrecks teams and friendships.

Luke 22:24-27

24 The apostles got into an argument about which one of them was the greatest. 25 So Jesus told them: "Foreign kings order their people around, and powerful rulers call themselves everyone's friends. 26 But don't be like them. The most important one of you should be like the least important, and your leader should be like a servant. 27 Who do people think is the greatest, a person who is served or one who serves? Isn't it the one who is served? But I have been with you as a servant."

Prayer: Take a minute or two to think of a time when you were bossy. Talk to God about this and ask him to forgive you. Think of someone who upsets you because they are bossy. Pray for them that they will not be so selfish.

An extra idea

Congratulations! You are doing well. You have read a lot of Luke's Gospel. Keep going.

We haven't room in this Hotshots book to read all of Luke. In the next few pages we'll be reading about how Jesus died and came back to life again. We have to leave some of it out.

You might like to read the bits of the story we have left out. You could ask your parents to read these with you.

First, here's a section about the night Jesus was arrested.

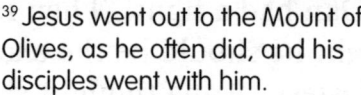

Luke 22:39-53

39 Jesus went out to the Mount of Olives, as he often did, and his disciples went with him.

41 Jesus walked on a little way before he knelt down and prayed, 42 "Father, if you will, please don't make me suffer by having me drink from this cup. But do what you want, and not what I want." 43 Then an angel from heaven came to help him. 44 Jesus was in great pain.

45 Jesus got up from praying and went over to his disciples. They were asleep and worn out from being so sad. 46 He said to them, "Why are you asleep? Wake up and pray that you won't be tested."

47 While Jesus was still speaking, a crowd came up. It was led by Judas, one of the twelve apostles. He went over to Jesus and greeted him with a kiss.

48 Jesus asked Judas, "Are you betraying the Son of Man with a kiss?"

49 When Jesus' disciples saw what was about to happen, they asked, "Lord, should we attack them with a sword?"
50 One of the disciples even struck at the high priest's servant with his sword and cut off the servant's right ear.

51 "Enough of that!" Jesus said. Then he touched the servant's ear and healed it.

52 Jesus spoke to the chief priests, the temple police, and the leaders who had come to arrest him. He said, "Why do you come out with swords and clubs and treat me like a criminal? 53 I was with you every day in the temple, and you didn't arrest me. But this is your time, and darkness is in control."

Prayer: *When you've finished, tell Jesus about how you feel about this story.*

Hotshots training session

Warming up & cooling down

Some tips :

1. Start slowly and gently, walking around then jogging on the spot – not fast at first.

2. Then a bit faster. Use a skipping rope for jumping and skipping. Wave your arms.

3. Start bending – reaching high and bending low.

4. And stretching – push against a wall or tree.

5. Keep breathing slowly, steadily and easily.

6. Do several sit ups – reaching towards your toes then reach back till your back is flat on the ground.

7. Keep moving until you're slightly uncomfortable but not in pain.

8. Now you're ready!

Peter trips

Chris was still in a bad mood because of the argument about who should be captain. He threw the basketball around without caring where it went and broke a window. Jeff asked who threw the ball. Chris blamed Samuel swearing about it loudly. Most people guessed it was really Chris but kept quiet and looked the other way. Samuel protested.

Jesus' friend, Peter, had a similar experience. The more he told lies, the more upset he became. Read the story.

Luke 22:54-61

54 Jesus was arrested and led away to the house of the high priest, while Peter followed at a distance. 55 Some people built a fire in the middle of the courtyard and were sitting around it. Peter sat there with them, 56 and a servant girl saw him. Then after she had looked at him carefully, she said, "This man was with Jesus!"

57 Peter said, "Woman, I don't even know that man!" 58 A little later someone else saw Peter and said, "You are one of them!" "No, I'm not!" Peter replied.

59 About an hour later another man insisted, "This man must have been with Jesus. They both come from Galilee."

Peter trips (continued ...)

⁶⁰ Peter replied, "I don't know what you are talking about!" At once, while Peter was still speaking, a rooster crowed.

⁶¹ The Lord turned and looked at Peter. And Peter remembered that the Lord had said, "Before a rooster crows tomorrow morning, you will say three times that you don't know me." ⁶²Then Peter went out and cried hard.

Prayer: Lord Jesus, please help me to be brave about following you.

Use this bag of words to say how you feel about this story. Choose a word to fill in the missing spaces.

feeling guilty
curious ashamed
sad heart-broken foolish
afraid
embarrassed

In verse 54, I think Peter was

_____

In verse 57, I think Peter was

_____

In verse 58, I think Peter was

_____

In verse 60, I think Peter was

_____

In verse 62, I think Peter was

_____

Some more extra ideas

Just as you began reading some extra parts of the story, here is a section about the terrible time Jesus had when he was taken to the court. People made up all sorts of lies about him. Some people thought it was a joke but it was too cruel to be funny. Tick each block when you have finished it.

❏ The police have cruel fun

Luke 22:63-65

63 The men who were guarding Jesus made fun of him and beat him. 64 They put a blindfold on him and said, "Tell us who struck you!" 65 They kept on insulting Jesus in many other ways.

❏ The leaders get their chance

Luke 22:66-71

66 At daybreak the nation's leaders, the chief priests, and the teachers of the Law of Moses got together and brought Jesus before their council. 67 They said, "Tell us! Are you the Messiah?"

Jesus replied, "If I said so, you wouldn't believe me. 68 And if I asked you a question, you wouldn't answer. 69 But from now on, the Son of Man will be seated at the right side of God All-Powerful."

70 Then they asked, "Are you the Son of God?" Jesus answered, "You say I am!"

71 They replied, "Why do we need more witnesses? He said it himself!"

❏ The governor gets confused

Luke 23:1-5

1 Everyone in the council got up and led Jesus off to Pilate. 2 They started accusing him and said, "We caught this man trying to get our people to riot and to stop paying taxes to the Emperor. He also claims that he is the Messiah, our king."

³ Pilate asked Jesus, "Are you the king of the Jews?" "Those are your words," Jesus answered.

⁴ Pilate told the chief priests and the crowd, "I don't find him guilty of anything."

⁵ But they all kept on saying, "He has been teaching and causing trouble all over Judea. He started in Galilee and has now come all the way here."

HE CLAIMS HE IS THE MESSIAH!

❑ The king's cruel fun

Luke 23:6-12

⁶ When Pilate heard this, he asked, "Is this man from Galilee?" ⁷ After Pilate learned that Jesus came from the region ruled by Herod, he sent him to Herod, who was in Jerusalem at that time.

⁸ For a long time Herod had wanted to see Jesus and was very happy because he finally had this chance. He had heard many things about Jesus and hoped to see him work a miracle.

⁹ Herod asked him a lot of questions, but Jesus did not answer. ¹⁰ Then the chief priests and the teachers of the Law of Moses stood up and accused him of all kinds of bad things.

¹¹ Herod and his soldiers made fun of Jesus and insulted him. They put a fine robe on him and sent him back to Pilate. ¹² That same day Herod and Pilate became friends, even though they had been enemies before this.

It's not fair!

The Hotshots couldn't stand it any longer. They knew that Chris broke the window and they all spoke at once to Jeff. Chris felt really, really terrible. And Samuel was glad the truth was known.

Jeff knew that something had to be done. It wouldn't be fair if Chris didn't accept the blame. Jeff talked quietly to Chris and asked him to pay some of his pocket money towards repairs. In the end everyone felt this was fair. Even Chris was glad that there was a way to put things right.

However the story of Jesus was not fair at all. The leaders were dishonest and became more and more cruel.

Luke 23:13-25

¹³ Pilate called together the chief priests, the leaders, and the people. ¹⁴ He told them, "You brought Jesus to me and said he was a troublemaker. But I've questioned him here in front of you, and I haven't found him guilty of anything that you say he has done. ¹⁵ Herod didn't find him guilty either and sent him back. This man doesn't deserve to be put to death! ¹⁶⁻¹⁷ I'll just have him beaten with a whip and set free."

¹⁸ But the whole crowd shouted, "Kill Jesus! Give us Barabbas!" ¹⁹ Now Barabbas was in jail because he had started a riot in the city and had murdered someone.

²⁰ Pilate wanted to set Jesus free, so he spoke again to the crowds. ²¹ But they kept shouting, "Nail him to a cross! Nail him to a cross!"

²² Pilate spoke to them a third time, "But what crime has he done? I've not found him guilty of anything for which he should be put to death. I'll have him beaten with a whip and set free."

²³ The people kept on shouting as loud as they could for Jesus to be put to death. ²⁴ Finally, Pilate gave in. ²⁵ He freed the man who was in jail for rioting and murder, because he was the one the crowd wanted to be set free. Then Pilate handed Jesus over for them to do what they wanted with him.

We hope and expect judges, police and courts to be fair but sometimes they aren't. They weren't for Jesus. The governor said Jesus was 'not guilty', but he still gave in to the yelling mob.

Here is a graffiti board. Write down some things that make you angry because they are not fair. Write one thing about the trial of Jesus.

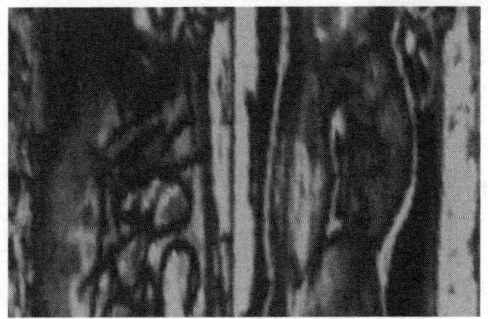

Prayer: Turn your graffiti into a prayer to tell God how you feel.

Now write in the empty speech bubble how Chris may feel now that the window problem is finished. Here are some ideas: 'That feels better', 'I won't do that again', 'We're friends again'.

52 Horrible and beautiful

When Chris paid for the window, Jeff arranged for a handyman to fix the glass. Jeff then told everyone: 'I've forgiven Chris. I know what he did was silly and wrong. Chris knows that too. But everything is finished now.'

The day when Jesus was nailed to the wooden cross on 'Skull Hill' was horrible. People were cruel and insulting.

Luke 23:26, 32-35

26 As Jesus was being led away, some soldiers grabbed hold of a man from Cyrene named Simon. He was coming in from the fields, but they put the cross on him and made him carry it behind Jesus.

32 Two criminals were led out to be put to death with Jesus. 33 When the soldiers came to the place called "The Skull," they nailed Jesus to a cross. They also nailed the two criminals to crosses, one on each side of Jesus.

34-35 Jesus said, "Father, forgive these people! They don't know what they're doing."

Jesus did something beautiful – he prayed for those who hurt him. See verse 34.

Jesus' enemies did not realise that they were killing God's Son. But because of his death, everyone everywhere can be forgiven. Jesus paid the price. We start by being sorry for our sin.

Prayer: Thank Jesus for dying for you.

53

A sad day

Emily came to Hotshots with sad news. 'My granny died. We really miss her.' The Hotshots talked together and tried to help Emily feel better.

Has anyone you know died? How did people show they were sad? Read about Jesus' death.

Luke 23:44-49

44 Around midday the sky turned dark and stayed that way until the middle of the afternoon. 45 The sun stopped shining, and the curtain in the temple split down the middle. 46 Jesus shouted, "Father, I put myself in your hands!" Then he died.

47 When the Roman officer saw what had happened, he praised God and said, "Jesus must really have been a good man!"

48 A crowd had gathered to see the terrible sight. Then after they had seen it, they felt broken-hearted and went home. 49 All of Jesus' close friends and the women who had come with him from Galilee stood at a distance and watched.

When Jesus died, people showed their sadness in different ways.

• Who praised God that Jesus was such a good man (verse 47)?

_____

• Who felt broken-hearted and went home (verse 48)?

_____

• Who stood a little way off and watched (verse 49)?

_____

Imagine how you would feel.
What would you do? Talk to God about it.

Relaxing and waiting

When her Granny died, Emily picked some flowers to give to her mother who felt sad about losing her mother. She found her favourite photos of Granny and made sure Granny's dog got fed. Some friends of Jesus did special things for him because they loved him.

Luke 23:50-56

50-51 There was a man named Joseph, who was from Arimathea in Judea. Joseph was a good and honest man, and he was eager for God's kingdom to come. He was also a member of the council, but he didn't agree with what they had decided.

52 Joseph went to Pilate and asked for Jesus' body. 53 He took the body down from the cross and wrapped it in fine cloth. Then he put it in a tomb that had been cut out of solid rock and had never been used. 54 It was Friday, and the Sabbath was about to begin.

55 The women who had come with Jesus from Galilee followed Joseph and watched how Jesus' body was placed in the tomb. 56 Then they went to prepare some sweet-smelling spices for his burial. But on the Sabbath they rested, as the Law of Moses commands.

Think about those who did special things for Jesus.

- Who lovingly put Jesus' body in a cave grave (verses 50 & 53)?

_____

- Who prepared perfume to put on Jesus' body (verses 55-56)?

_____

At first people were so sad they didn't think about why Jesus should have to die. But later they realised that he died for them and everyone else too. It was his way of forgiving everyone's sin.

- What is the special name for the day Jesus died?

  _____

- Many churches call the next day 'Holy Saturday'. Is this a good name? What would you call it?

  _____

Prayer: Thank you Lord Jesus for dying for me.

Can you decode this message?

Clue: 123 = for;   45 = en

wh45 you're 123giv45 it's 123gott45 123 good!

_____

_____

Hotshots training session

Cooling down slowly

After a match or a training session, take a couple of minutes to cool down.
- your body will get cooler gradually
- you will begin to relax
- you have less chance of feeling stiff and sore
- you can think and talk about the game.

Some tips :
1. Shake hands with the other team and say thank you.
2. Thank the umpire and your coach.
3. Put on some warm clothes again.
4. Keep moving around – not fast, just gently jogging and walking.
5. Stretch your body by pushing against a tree or wall until you can count to 20. Then lift one leg till you can count to 20; then the other leg.

55 Easter Day

How many feelings can you have in one day? The Hotshots remember one match when they felt hope, confusion, excitement, gladness and disappointment nearly all at once!

Find out what Jesus' friends experienced on Easter Day.

Luke 24:1-6

[1]Very early on Sunday morning the women went to the tomb, carrying the spices that they had prepared. [2] When they found the stone rolled away from the entrance, [3] they went in. But they didn't find the body of the Lord Jesus, [4] and they didn't know what to think.

Suddenly two men in shining white clothes stood beside them. [5] The women were afraid and bowed to the ground. But the men said, "Why are you looking in the place of the dead for someone who is alive? [6] Jesus isn't here! He has been raised from death.

Now read the story again and fill in the gaps with the right expressions on the faces.

On Sunday morning the women still felt _____ that Jesus had died. When they arrived at his grave they were _____ .
Why was the stone rolled away? Where was Jesus' body? Suddenly they were _____ by two angels. They felt _____ and bowed down low. 'Jesus is alive!' the angels said.

Prayer: *Make up your own prayer telling Jesus how you feel that he's alive.*

Afraid

Sad

Surprised

Puzzled

56 Everything changes

Some people believe things more easily than others – even if they're not true. Some Hotshots could hardly believe it when they won their first match!

This Easter story is true, but not everyone could believe what had happened.

Luke 24:9-12

9-10 Mary Magdalene, Joanna, Mary the mother of James, and some other women were the ones who had gone to the tomb. When they returned, they told the eleven apostles and the others what had happened. 11 The apostles thought it was all nonsense, and they wouldn't believe.

12 But Peter ran to the tomb. And when he stooped down and looked in, he saw only the burial clothes. Then he returned, wondering what had happened.

Amazed   Glad

Angry   Curious

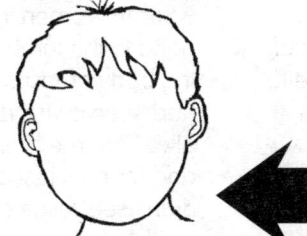

Let's keep going with the face expressions! Keep writing the words in the gaps.

The women hurried back to tell Jesus' friends. They thought the women's story was nonsense! This made the women feel _____ but Peter was _____ . He ran to check.
It was true! He was _____ .
Soon the friends met Jesus. They were _____ that Jesus was alive.

Prayer: Draw your own face showing how you feel that Jesus is alive.

57 Jesus comes near

Jeff invited the Hotshots to take part in a survey.
But first they had to read the Bible story.

Luke 24:13-24

13 That same day two of Jesus' disciples were going to the village of Emmaus, which was about 12 kilometres from Jerusalem. 14 As they were talking and thinking about what had happened, 15 Jesus came near and started walking along beside them. 16 But they didn't know who he was.

17 Jesus asked them, "What were you talking about as you walked along?"

The two of them stood there looking sad and gloomy. 18 Then the one named Cleopas asked Jesus, "Are you the only person from Jerusalem who doesn't know what was happening there these last few days?"

19 "What do you mean?" Jesus asked. They answered: "Those things that happened to Jesus from Nazareth. By what he did and said he showed that he was a powerful prophet, who pleased God and all the people. 20 Then the chief priests and our leaders had him arrested and sentenced to die on a cross.

21 We had hoped that he would be the one to set Israel free! But it has already been three days since all this happened.

22 Some women in our group surprised us. They had gone to the tomb early in the morning, 23 but didn't find the body of Jesus. They came back, saying that they had seen a vision of angels who told them that he is alive. 24 Some men from our group went to the tomb and found it just as the women had said. But they didn't see Jesus either."

Jesus came near his two friends.
They told him their sad story.
But they didn't know who he was.

Jesus is with us all the time, but
sometimes he seems much closer.
Fill in the survey.
The first row of boxes is
for you to do yourself.

The second row is for an
adult friend. Choose carefully someone
who would like to do it with you – your
Mum, your Dad or another adult friend.
Choose a good time to ask.

Prayer: *Lord Jesus, please help me to get
close to you.*

Survey

Please tick the ways that Jesus
seems closer to you:

Through:	*You*	*A friend*
• my family	❏	❏
• a friend	❏	❏
• my church or Sunday school	❏	❏
• a special program like a holiday club	❏	❏
• my school	❏	❏
• the Bible	❏	❏
• this Hotshots book	❏	❏
• another book	❏	❏
• something that happened to me	❏	❏
• another way - _____	❏	❏

Talking about the Bible

Each time the Hotshots met, they read a Bible story. This time they felt they were exploring the Bible with two friends from long ago.

Luke 24:27-35

27 Jesus then explained everything written about himself in the Scriptures, beginning with the Law of Moses and the Books of the Prophets.

28 When the two of them came near the village where they were going, Jesus seemed to be going further. 29 They begged him, "Stay with us! It's already late, and the sun is going down." So Jesus went into the house to stay with them.

30 After Jesus sat down to eat, he took some bread. He blessed it and broke it. Then he gave it to them. 31 At once they knew who he was, but he disappeared. 32 They said to each other, "When he talked with us along the road and explained the Scriptures to us, didn't it warm our hearts?" 33 So they got right up and returned to Jerusalem. The two disciples found the eleven apostles and the others gathered together. 34 And they learnt from the group that the Lord was really alive and had appeared to Peter. 35 Then the disciples from Emmaus told them what happened on the road and how they knew he was the Lord when he broke the bread.

Jesus and his friends didn't have a Bible. They were too poor to own one. But they did know lots about the Bible. Then Jesus helped them to understand it. Read verse 32 to see how they felt.

He showed them that everything hadn't gone terribly wrong. Hundreds of years before, the prophets who wrote the Old Testament said that the Messiah would die and come alive again. Jesus really was the Messiah – God's Son.

Did you know? 'Scriptures' means the Bible. But then only the Old Testament part was written.

On the map picture, draw footsteps to show how many people walked along the road. Show the way they went.

Panting and breathless they raced back to Jerusalem and hammered on the doors. 'He's alive!' they said.

Now draw another set of footsteps on the picture map to show how many people raced back along the road. Show the way they went.

Prayer: *Dear God, thank you for the stories in the Bible. Thank you that I can read it.*

Did you know?

- Luke wrote another book – called 'Acts' about what happened after the stories in his Gospel.

- Matthew, Mark and John also wrote Gospels. Some of their stories are the same and some are different.

- In the Bible there is a book of Psalms. This was the hymn book Jesus and his friends used. Can you find it in your Bible?

- Scripture Union prints other books to help people of all ages to read the Bible. Maybe there are some books which will help other members of your family.

If you are growing too old for Hotshots ...

try *Snapshots!*

There's a Bible section for every day. There are puzzles and activities.

You can subscribe to receive Snapshots every quarter.

Near the end

You have met the Hotshots and learnt about Jesus from Luke's Gospel. How do you feel? Tick the boxes.

❏ Sad ❏ Sorry ❏ Satisfied ❏ Glad ❏ Want more

Did you tick all the boxes? That's how Jesus' friends felt when he came to see them for the last time. Read the verses below and fill in the gaps.

Their mood changed from _____ and

_____ (verse 37) to _____

and _____ (verse 41).

Luke 24:36-43

36 While Jesus' disciples were talking about what had happened, Jesus appeared and greeted them. 37 They were frightened and terrified because they thought they were seeing a ghost.

38 But Jesus said, "Why are you so frightened? Why do you doubt? 39 Look at my hands and my feet and see who I am! Touch me and find out for yourselves. Ghosts don't have flesh and bones as you see I have."

40 After Jesus said this, he showed them his hands and his feet. 41 The disciples were so glad and amazed that they couldn't believe it. Jesus then asked them, "Have you got something to eat?" 42 They gave him a piece of baked fish. 43 He took it and ate it as they watched.

By dying and coming back to life again, Jesus has made a way for us to be forgiven and have a fresh start as his friends and followers.

We can thank Jesus for his special love and ask him to help us obey what he teaches us.

Prayer: Make your own prayer asking Jesus to help you be a good friend and follower.

Celebrations

The Hotshots had come to the end of one season and soon would begin a new one. It was time to celebrate! The hall was filled with balloons and all kinds of yummy food. The 'Most Improved Player' was awarded to Samuel. Everyone felt pleased. They all received a Hotshots Players Certificate. You will find one *for you* on page 96. Make a photocopy. Find a good spot for it.

Luke 24:46-53

46 He told them: "... beginning in Jerusalem, 48 you must tell everyone everything that has happened. 49 I will send you the one my Father has promised, but you must stay in the city until you are given power from heaven."

50 Jesus led his disciples out to Bethany, where he raised his hands and blessed them. 51 As he was doing this, he left and was taken up to heaven. 52 After his disciples had worshipped him, they returned to Jerusalem and were very happy. 53 They spent their time in the temple, praising God.

Jesus' friends had a strange feeling. Their adventure with Jesus was finishing. But when he told them his Spirit would be with them wherever they went, they felt their adventure was only beginning. No one could be sad then.

The Holy Spirit is not spooky or weird. He is sometimes called 'the Spirit of Christ' to show everyone that it is Jesus – still alive, and living with us.

The Holy Spirit did come. Read about it in the next chapter by Luke – Acts chapter 1.

Prayer: *Lord Jesus, please help me to keep on growing in my friendship with you. Help me to be my best for you.*

Now you have finished this Hotshots book it is a good idea to think about the things that you have read.

* Which member of the Hotshots team would you like to meet

_____

* Did anything surprise you about Jesus in this book?

_____

* What did you think of the ideas in this book?
  ❏ Hard to understand   ❏ Great fun
  ❏ Helpful   ❏ Interesting
  ❏ Not really good

* When you were reading this book, did you decide there is something you should do in your life?

_____

_____

How to begin following Jesus

The **Hotshots** have been finding out about lots of people who became followers of Jesus. They were like a big family of friends.

Some followers were fishermen. Turn back to page 12 and write down the names of three of them.

_____   _____   _____

Some were women. Turn back to page 40 and write down the names of two of them.

_____   _____

These days Jesus still invites people to follow him.

Here is why the **Hotshots** follow Jesus . . .

How to begin following Jesus

The first steps

Deciding whether to follow Jesus is like answering an invitation to a party. Look at Jesus' story on page 54.

Begin a new life with Jesus with a prayer like this. Read these words carefully. Make up your own prayer saying 'thank you', 'sorry' and 'please'.

> Jesus invites <u>everyone</u> to be his friends and followers. Some people say yes, but others don't accept.

Step One

Thank you

Say thank you to God for loving you and for his promise to forgive you. Thank him for Jesus who came to show us the way and how to get rid of our sin.

Step Two

Sorry

Tell God you are sorry for the sin and wrong in your life. Ask him to forgive you.

Step Three

Please

Ask God to live in your life and give you a new beginning. Ask for his help to do what he says. Say a prayer like this in your own words. Write it on a piece of paper.

If you really mean what you say, you can be sure God hears you and that you're now part of Jesus' family.

Write the date you prayed this prayer:

_____

Certificate

Scripture
Union
and

The
Hotshots
Team

This is to certify that

_____

(write you name neatly)

has completed the stories and projects from Luke's Gospel
using 'The world's greatest leader – ever!'

Signed: ....*Jeff*..................................Jeff   (Hotshots Coach)

Countersigned:...(Parent or other adult)

Date:..